BLAZERS

ALL ABOUT FANTASY CREATURES

Discover
ORCS,
BOGGARTS,
AND
Other Nasty
Fantasy Creatures

by A.J. Sautter

CAPSTONE PRESS
a capstone imprint

Blazers Books are published by Capstone Press,
1710 Roe Crest Drive, North Mankato, Minnesota 56003
www.mycapstone.com

Library of Congress Cataloging-in-Publication data
Names: Sautter, Aaron, author.
Title: Discover orcs, boggarts, and other nasty fantasy creatures / by A.J. Sautter.
Description: Mankato, Minnesota : Capstone Press, [2018] | Series: Blazers. all about
   fantasy creatures | Includes bibliographical references and index.
Summary: "In handbook format, describes the physical features, behavior, and
   habitat of nasty fantasy creatures"—Provided by publisher.
Identifiers: LCCN 2017002067 (print) | LCCN 2017014760 (ebook) |
   ISBN 9781515768548 (eBook PDF) | ISBN 9781515768371 (library hardcover) |
   ISBN 9781515768418 (paperback)
Subjects: LCSH: Animals, Mythical—Juvenile literature. | Monsters—Juvenile literature.
Classification: LCC GR825 (ebook) | LCC GR825 .S276 2018 (print) |
   DDC 398/.45—dc23
LC record available at https://lccn.loc.gov/2017002067

Editorial Credits
Bobbie Nuytten, designer; Wanda Winch, media researcher;
Laura Manthe, production specialist

Photo Credits
Capstone: Colin Ashcroft, 4, 28, Collin Howard, 17, 25, 27, Jason Juta, 3, 19, 21, Martin
Bustamante, cover (bottom left, right), 1 (right), 7, 9, 11, 13, Stefano Azzalin, 5, 32, Tom
McGrath, 15, 23; Shutterstock: Carlos Caetano, cover (background), 1 (background)

Printed in the United States of America.
010364F17

TABLE OF CONTENTS

NASTY FANTASY CREATURES!

Fantasy tales feature many nasty creatures. Wicked orcs, hags, and others cause a lot of trouble for heroes. What would these creatures be like if they were real? Where and how would they live? Let's look deeper to find out!

Fact: People long ago believed that fantasy creatures were real. When mysterious things happened, they often blamed it on wicked fantasy creatures.

Black Orcs

Size: 6.5 to 7 feet (2 to 2.1 meters) tall
Home: mountain caves or strong fortresses
Diet: rats, mountain goats, dwarves, humans
Lifespan: unknown

Appearance: Black orcs are big and strong. Their tough skin is often marked with battle scars. They have yellow eyes, pointed ears, and greasy black hair. Their mouths are full of jagged teeth and fangs.

crossbow—a type of bow that is held and fired with a trigger like a gun

catapult—a weapon used to hurl large rocks or other objects at enemies

Behavior: Evil wizards grow black orcs in special underground chambers. These creatures are violent, cruel, and short-tempered. Black orcs are highly-skilled warriors. They often use complex weapons, such as **crossbows** and **catapults**.

Boggarts

Size: 8 to 12 inches (20 to 30 centimeters) tall
Home: closets, attics, and other small spaces in old houses
Diet: stale bread, sour milk, moldy cheese, old food scraps
Lifespan: unknown

Appearance: Boggarts are a wicked form of brownies. They are bigger and stronger than brownies and have green skin. They have black eyes, pointed ears, and coarse whiskers. A boggart's mouth is full of nasty, sharp teeth.

Behavior: Brownies turn into nasty boggarts if they become angry. Boggarts never kill. But they enjoy breaking things, playing pranks, and causing problems. Anyone who insults a boggart should apologize. It will then return to its friendly brownie form.

GOBLINS

Size: 4 to 4.5 feet (1.2 to 1.4 m) tall
Home: deep, dark mountain caves
Diet: worms, insects, mushrooms, rats, gnomes
Lifespan: 20 to 25 years

Appearance: Goblins are often mistaken for orcs. But they are smaller and usually walk in a bent over position. Goblins have pointed ears, large yellow eyes, and sharp jagged teeth.

Behavior: Goblins never leave their dark caves during the day. They don't produce their own food. They instead **raid** farms and villages for what they need. However, goblins often create clever traps and weapons to defend their homes.

> **raid**—to make a sudden, surprise attack on a place

GREMLINS

Size: 2 to 2.5 feet (0.6 to 0.8 m) tall
Home: deep, dark underground caves
Diet: worms, insects, snails, salamanders
Lifespan: 5 to 6 years

Appearance: Gremlins usually have scaly green skin. Their large eyes are often blue, but can be yellow, green, or red. They have jagged teeth and long sharp **talons**. Their huge ears are shaped like a bat's wings.

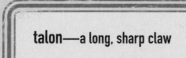

talon—a long, sharp claw

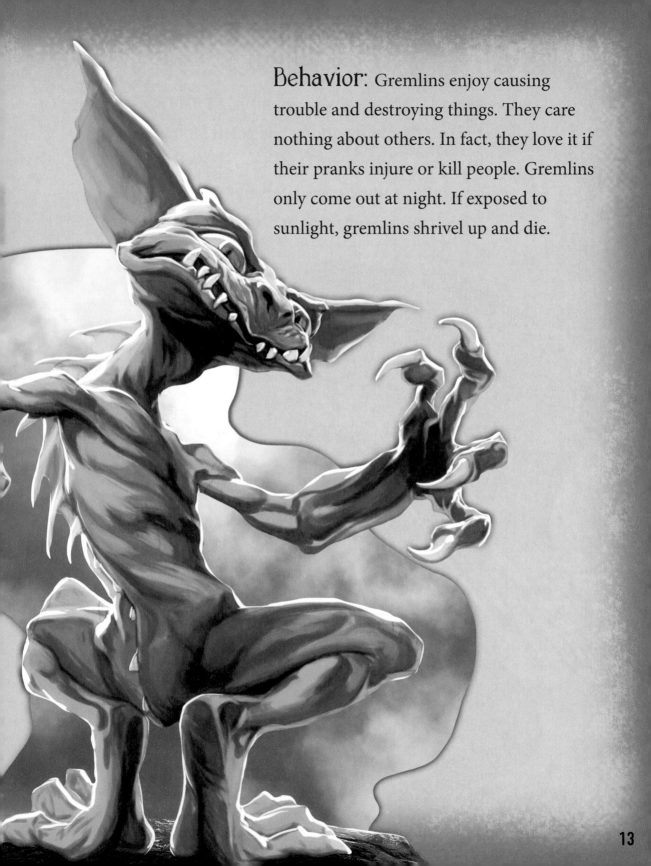

Behavior: Gremlins enjoy causing trouble and destroying things. They care nothing about others. In fact, they love it if their pranks injure or kill people. Gremlins only come out at night. If exposed to sunlight, gremlins shrivel up and die.

HAGS

Size: 5.5 to 6 feet (1.7 to 1.8 m) tall
Home: damp caves or ruined old shacks
Diet: worms, snails, slugs, toads, rats, humans
Lifespan: unknown

Appearance: Hags look like hideous old women. They have thin bodies, hunched backs, and stringy hair. Their green skin is often covered in hairy warts. They have long pointed noses and black, rotting teeth.

> **lair**—a hideout used by wicked people to keep their activities secret

Behavior: Hags affect the lands where they live. Forests and wetlands become dead and rotten. Hags have a strong craving for human flesh. They use magic spells to lure people into their dark **lairs**. There they can satisfy their hunger.

HOBGOBLINS

Size: 5.5 to 6 feet (1.7 to 1.8 m) tall
Home: mountain caves or ruined stone castles
Diet: rabbits, sheep, goats, gnomes, goblins, dwarves
Lifespan: about 35 years

Appearance: Hobgoblins are covered in coarse brown or black hair. Most have red eyes and two sharp tusks in their lower jaws. Many hobgoblins wear bits of bone or metal in their beards.

Behavior: Hobgoblins value military training. Children begin training as soon as they can hold a sword. Hobgoblins often use complex weapons like crossbows. They are tireless fighters. During battles, they keep fighting until they win or are killed.

Nixies

Size: 4 to 4.5 feet (1.2 to 1.4 m) tall
Home: warm freshwater ponds and lakes
Diet: fish, clams, frogs, water plants
Lifespan: unknown, possibly up to 400 years

Appearance: Nixies hatch from eggs and grow like tadpoles. Their arms, legs, and flipperlike feet grow out as they get older. Nixies have pale green skin covered with fishlike scales. Instead of ears, nixies have **gills** to breathe underwater.

gill—a body part used to breathe underwater
illusion—something that appears to be real but isn't

Behavior: Nixies normally use **illusions** to keep people away from their homes. However, some nixies are more wicked. They use their magic to trap people and use them as slaves.

ORCS

Size: 4.5 to 5 feet (1.4 to 1.5 m) tall

Home: mountain caves and deserted castles

Diet: rats, squirrels, rabbits, deer, humans, elves

Lifespan: about 50 years

Appearance: Orcs can have black, brown, gray, or pale white skin. Some have long greasy hair. Others have no hair at all. Most orcs are ugly and have squinty eyes, pointed ears, and jagged teeth.

Behavior: Orcs hate nature and beautiful artwork. They hate elves most of all. Orcs are related to black orcs, but are shorter and weaker. They are cruel and have violent tempers. Orcs are also not very smart. But they often make clever weapons and armor from wood and bone.

PIXIES

Size: 6 to 8 inches (15 to 20 cm) tall
Home: hollow trees and logs
Diet: seeds, nuts, wild berries, mushrooms, honey
Lifespan: about 300 years

Appearance: Pixies look similar to small fairies. Pixies have large eyes, pointed ears, and butterfly-like wings. They usually have black or dark brown hair. Their clothing is often made from dead leaves or grass.

Behavior: Pixies like to explore the world. They enjoy stealing small items like thimbles, toothpicks, and string. Pixies enjoy playing tricks on people. But their pranks often go too far. People sometimes get hurt.

SIRENS

Size: 6 to 6.5 feet (1.8 to 2 m) long

Home: rocky islands and ocean coastlines

Diet: fish, oysters, sea urchins, starfish, octopuses, human sailors

Lifespan: up to 1,000 years

Appearance: Sirens look like monstrous mermaids. They have scaly yellow-green skin and clawed hands. Their fins are often red or blue. Sirens have sharp, needlelike teeth. They use their strong tails for fast swimming.

prey—an animal hunted by another animal for food

Behavior: Sirens are also known as sea hags. They use magic to trick sailors at sea. Sailors believe the sirens are beautiful women calling from shore. The sailors often smash their ships on nearby rocks. Then sirens can easily capture their foolish **prey**.

TROGLODYTES

Size: 5 to 5.5 feet (1.5 to 1.7 m) tall

Home: damp, underground caves or dark swamps

Diet: fish, frogs, snakes, birds, muskrats, humans

Lifespan: up to 130 years

Appearance: Most troglodytes have scaly green skin. Their jaws are filled with razor-sharp teeth. They have powerful tails like an alligator's. Males have colorful **frills** on their heads and necks. Some people think troglodytes are a type of **humanoid** dragon.

frill—a flap of skin on a reptile's head or neck

humanoid—shaped somewhat like a human

sacrifice—something valuable that is offered to a god; often a living creature is killed to honor the god

Behavior: Troglodytes are strong and fierce fighters. They often raid villages to steal food, weapons, treasure, and people. Captives are used as slaves, food, or **sacrifices** to the Troglodytes' gods.

Creature Quiz

1. Which of the following do orcs hate the most?

   A) gnomes

   B) elves

   C) pixies

2. If you're on a ship and see a beautiful woman singing and waving to you from shore, it is likely a:

   A) siren.

   B) nixie.

   C) gorgon.

3. Gremlins are best known for:

   A) creating clever weapons and traps.

   B) playing pranks and destroying things.

   C) raiding villages to steal food.

4. The best way to deal with a troublesome boggart is to:

   A) expose it to sunlight.

   B) offer it money to leave you alone.

   C) apologize for any insults.

5. Troglodytes often raid villages to steal:

   A) food and weapons.

   B) treasure and people.

   C) all of the above.

6. Which wicked creatures make the best warriors?

  A) goblins

  B) black orcs

  C) troglodytes

7. How do hags catch their victims?

  A) They use magic to lure people into their homes.

  B) They steal children during the night.

  C) They use a magic sleeping potion.

8. How are black orcs created?

  A) They are born as babies.

  B) They are made magically.

  C) They are grown underground in special chambers.

9. As nixies age, they grow:

  A) fins and tails like a fish.

  B) legs, arms, and feet like tadpoles do.

  C) claws like a crab or lobster.

10. As pixies explore the world they like to:

  A) collect small trinkets like toothpicks and thimbles.

  B) play pranks on people for fun.

  C) both A and B.

See page 31 for quiz answers.

Glossary

catapult (KAT-uh-puhlt)—a weapon used to hurl large rocks or other objects at enemies

crossbow (KRAWS-boh)—a type of bow that is held and fired with a trigger like a gun

frill (FRIL)—a flap of skin on a reptile's head or neck

gill (GIL)—a body part used to breathe underwater

humanoid (HYOO-muh-noyd)—shaped somewhat like a human

illusion (i-LOO-zhuhn)—something that appears to be real but isn't

lair (LAYR)—a hideout used by wicked people to keep their activities secret

prey (PRAY)—an animal hunted by another animal for food

raid (RAYD)—to make a sudden, surprise attack on a place

sacrifice (SAK-ruh-fisse)—something valuable that is offered to a god; often a living creature is killed to honor the god

talon (TAL-uhn)—a long, sharp claw

Read More

Forbeck, Matt. *Dungeonology.* Ologies. Somerville, Mass.: Candlewick Press, 2016.

Loewen, Nancy. *Trust Me, Hansel and Gretel Are Sweet!: The Story of Hansel and Gretel as Told by the Witch.* The Other Side of the Story. North Mankato, Minn.: Picture Window Books, 2016.

Sautter, A. J. *How to Draw Orcs, Goblins, and Other Wicked Creatures.* Drawing Fantasy Creatures. North Mankato, Minn.: Capstone Press, 2016.

Quiz Answers:

1:B, 2:A, 3:B, 4:C, 5:C, 6:B, 7:A, 8:C, 9:B, 10:C

Internet Sites

Use FactHound to find Internet sites related to this book.

Visit *www.facthound.com*

Just type in 9781515768371 and go.

Check out projects, games and lots more at **www.capstonekids.com**

Index